nF418131

Through it all,
I see yellow.

About the Author:
My name is Grace Peck and I was born and raised in Eagan, MN. I attended college in Duluth, MN where I graduated with a Bachelor of Science in Nursing. While I am passionate about helping people through the medical field, I find my words to be more powerful than my actions. I wrote these poems and this book throughout the last several years of my life as a way to help me overcome some of the traumas life has thrown my way. I hope some of what I say resonates with you and helps you the way it has helped me. At the end of the day, you will make it through the battles life throws at you, and through it all- I hope you see yellow.

Dedicated to:
My loved ones who helped me stay to
stay positive during the challenges of
life.

I always write poems about the people
who hurt me,
and I could fill a fucking book with the
ones about you.

I offered you my hand,
a thousand times over,
to pull you out from the depths,
of the darkest parts of yourself,
you were too scared,
of the unknown,
you wanted me to join you,
because suffering is much easier,
when you're not alone,
I thought you needed a friend,
that I could be your light
at the end of the tunnel,
but you disguised your selfishness,
with the promise that I would receive
your love,
as long as your problems became my
blame,
but it will forever be my fault for
forgiving you,
time and time again,
and never your fault,
for disguising your depression,
as the road that led to your heart,
I guess I was so captivated by healing
you,
I didn't realize,

I was giving you my health to do it.

In the end,
I have no regrets,
I don't regret convincing myself to see
the good in you,
even when you showed me none at all,
I don't regret helping you,
even when it was never reciprocated,
I don't regret staying,
in your house of self-hatred,
fighting with you to open up the
windows and let light in,
just for you to close them,
time and time again,
I don't regret handing you the knife,
you continuously used to stab me in the
back,
and I don't regret loving you,
because if someone can love you,
through hell and high water,
then you are capable of being loved,
through anything,
and if I helped you realize the love you
deserve,
why would I regret anything?

I wanted so badly,
to make you happy,
so,
I tried to get you to love me,
unfortunately,
they aren't always the same thing.

You cared about your excuses,
and your reasons for hurting me,
more than you cared about actually
hurting me,
my tears triggered your defense
mechanism,
and not your empathetic response,
and I am still just trying to figure out
who I was,
before you broke my heart,
by teaching me that meant that you
loved me,
and oh honey,
fuck you for that.

Home can be a person,
but just because you were my home,
doesn't mean I was happy there,
I just thought having a home,
was better than not having one,
but the second I stepped outside,
I realized being homeless,
was so much better,
than being trapped in your home.

You stabbed me in the back,
but I would take the knife,
and give it back to you,
knowing damn well,
you'll just do it over and over again,
because the split second,
that I get to look into your eyes,
while I am giving you back,
the ability to hurt me,
is worth it,
because even if our love was toxic,
it was better to me,
than no love at all.

The weekend rolls around,
and we text each other drunk,
trying to hide the fact,
that our drunk thoughts,
should be our sober actions,
but we're both just too scared,
to be sober at all.

We met when the days were longer,
and my hair is a lot shorter now,
we fell in love fast,
but you broke me slow,
it started the seventh time you left,
and ended years later,
after I finally learned to cope with the
person you made me become.

You're mad because you think I blamed
all my scars on you,
but I know they're not from you.

I just expected you to help me heal
them,
instead of making them bigger.

And it is difficult,
it is so damn difficult,
when the only way you'd know the door
was shut,
was if I slammed it,
when the only way it could end,
was to burn down the house you locked
me in,
I didn't want it to be this way,
but I would rather be your enemy,
than let you end me,
and I simply couldn't keep defending a
love,
where all I ever did was defend myself.

I just wanted to fix you,
I wanted to show you the light at the
end of the tunnel,
and the flowers that can grow in the
depths of your mind,
and if I could turn my mind into a
mirror just so you could see the
reflection of how I view you,
I would in a heartbeat,
but it isn't my place to get cut by your
broken pieces,
you need to learn how to make the
edges duller,
I can't teach you to finish the puzzle
whose cover I've never seen,
I can't be an example of who you want
to be because I don't even know who
you are,
I wanted to make you love yourself,
in hopes that it would teach you how to
love me.

You said that you were changing,
you said you just needed time,
just wait until the end of summer,
and it'll all be fine,
fall came around,
and you were still singing the same
damn tune,
you said you just didn't like to be
wrong,
and that that's something I related to,
you claim you can empathize,
because you've seen the devil too,
but I've met him in person,
and not just in the mirror looking back
at me,
you said your lack of empathy,
was excused with the presence of
ignorance,
you said you just haven't walked in my
shoes,
but you shouldn't fucking have to,
your inability to commit to me,
never stemmed from your inability to
connect with me,
it came from your insecurity that I
knew you,

when you didn't even fucking know
you,
it came from your inability to be alone,
so, you jump from relationship to
relationship,
but still end up on my doorstep every
time,
I pray there's not a doorstep that comes
after mine.
you said that you were changing,
you said you just needed time,
but it's been a year,
and I'm still writing poems about you
on coffee shop tables,
on napkins,
and receipts,
and you're still writing the same damn
apology text,
telling me it'll be different,
it will never ever be different,
because you will never want me,
you'll want my presence and my hand
to hold
whenever you get lonely,
it will never be different,
because if you wanted to change for me,

you would have,
but you didn't,
fuck you.

I mistakenly confused your love of controlling me as your love for me.

When I was younger,
I promised myself I would never get
into a relationship,
with a man like my father,
but with his cassette stuffed into your
vocal chords,
I realized the words were calming,
the familiarity of reassurance that
change would come,
resonated well within my being,
I had walked these halls a million times,
why would I not want to follow them,
toward answers I wanted so badly to be
true,
I have read your book of lies,
but was always taught to read between
the lines,
those empty spaces you filled with
empty promises,
disguised as compromise,
if I didn't fight back we wouldn't fight,
it was me that loaded the gun, right?
it was my fault you shot me?
I am not tired of the endless arguments,
I am tired of them making me love you
more,

I am not sorry that I found comfort in
the walls of the house you claimed to
have built for me,
I was raised in the same house,
it just looks different from the outside,
I stayed because I wanted to change
you into the man,
I hoped my whole life that my father
would become,
but now I must leave,
because you will never fill shoes that
don't exist.

Sometimes I just wish you would've met
my mom,
so, she could tell me how she knows
you're not the one,
and remind me often of how much she
hated you,
cause I know she would have,
I wish you would've met my friends,
so, we can all laugh about you when
we're 25,
and I've moved on to a much better life,
I wish you would've come into my life,
instead of sat on the sidelines,
making me feel as if my sorrow over
you seems blown out of proportion,
and last but not least
I wish you would've met me and I mean
actually met me,
Not the 2 am version,
Or the version of me who drank a little
too much,
I mean the girl who paints and dances
in the rain,
the girl who cries at sunrises,
and the girl who wrote 1,000 too many
poems about you,

but you didn't
and I guess we will never know if it
would've worked if we would've met the
right versions of each other,
because all I ever did was tried to make
that happen,
and all you ever did was run from
anything that felt real.

I miss you but won't tell you,
because even if you'd say it back,
you don't miss me the way I miss you,
you miss the way our bodies fit together
like puzzle pieces,
but I miss your voice,
and way I could make a pillow out of
your words
when you spoke so softly,
and lie on it listening to you for hours,
you miss our drunk nights,
but I miss our mornings,
when the amber light hit the curves of
your face,
and lit up my world of you,
even if just for a minute,
so no,
I won't tell you,
because I miss you,
and you miss us,
I miss the piece you were,
and you miss feeling complete,
you just need someone to fill that hole,
and I need you.

You asked her why she stayed so long,
so, I know you don't understand
addiction,
you don't understand what it takes,
it's hard,
when someone feeds your addiction,
enough to make you stay,
but not enough to make you happy,
the second you try to leave,
they pull you back just enough,
that you forget how to open the door
and it just happens over and over
again,
until you're finally ready to leave,
and that's when they tell you they love
you.

1,000 poems crumpled up,
turned into messages in a bottle,
to be placed in the river,
that is your blood stream,
will still never make their way,
on the proper course towards your
heart,
like I wished so badly they would,
but simply make their way to your
shoulder,
where you brush them off so easily,
just like you did with me,
but my poor, romantic soul,
still wakes up hopes,
that maybe,
just maybe,
poem 1,001,
might just find its way.

You shouldn't need blurry vision
to think clearly about us.

I was the sun,
bright and full of life,
you were the moon,
dark and mysterious,
each were diminished,
when the other was around,
the constant fight between day and
night,
the power struggle,
and competition for the spotlight,
the utter curiosity,
of how one could be so different from
ourselves,
kept lighting our desire to understand.
but maybe the reason our paths
crossed,
was to make us realize that if day and
night became one,
well darling that is simply impossible,
unless we want to watch our world
burn.

I gave you the key to my heart,
and the ability to open it,
because I didn't think,
you would chisel it down,
into a knife,
and stab me in the back with it.

I hate how I am here,
rebuilding myself,
while you are putting on the same
mask,
to fool yet another woman.

You read my body as if I was written in braille,
but you didn't read my poems.

I don't care how long it takes,
I don't care how many poems I need to
write,
I don't care if it's a perfectly published
and complete manuscript, of
everything you've ever made me feel,
that is the answer to getting over you,
I'll write until my fingers are numb,
I'll write until I break both my thumbs,
to break out of these handcuffs,
of self-hatred that you locked my brain
in,
I will write until my poetry can build
me a bridge,
right over the river of my love for you,
I will write until I am no longer writing
the poems for you,
but for me.

I will no longer let the things you did to me influence the things I do to myself.

I loved you,
because you made me feel empowered,
because the chase was addicting,
and the rareness of your reciprocity,
always left me wanting more,
I loved you,
because you let me be the angel,
in the life you called hell,
in my version of the story,
you were the devil,
but it was my fault for letting you be
evil,
my fault for accepting your flaws,
and my fault for hoping you'd change,
but in the end,
it wasn't more faith I needed,
it was freedom.

I stayed because
taking care of
someone who felt worthless,
made me feel worthy.

I am drunk in love with someone who only loves me when they're drunk.

You didn't leave me with a piece to fill
you left me with wounds to heal.

I was just your type,
young and careless
with an open mind,
and you were just my type,
because you made me laugh enough to
forget the times you made me cry.

We always split the blame 50/50,
like the bill on the first date.

I'll sit here and convince myself I don't
miss you,
as I write poems and send them into the
oblivion,
hoping they'll land in your lap,
and you'll read them and run,
run until you get to me and hold me in
your arms,
I'll sit here and convince myself I don't
want you anymore,
as I open every new door,
in hopes they'll be a safe haven,
like there was when I opened yours,
I'll convince myself I'm over you,
because it was me that walked away,
but if you ever showed up at my
doorstep again,
my heart would be so happy,
even if I told you not to stay.

For self-love is hard,
for it's the hardest thing you'll ever do,
it takes intentionality,
a sunrise is much more beautiful than
the back of a pillow case,
but sometimes you need sleep,
hiking is more exciting than homework,
but it would make you stressed,
to leave it unfinished,
so, you should stay in,
see, self-love is different for all,
it really just means doing whatever you
want,
whatever will make you happy,
without worrying about outside
opinions,
but if you do not understand your
emotions and what will help you,
and if you do understand yourself,
then you will never love yourself,
so, take some time, and just be still.

Every time you walked out the door,
you made me realize how easy it was to
open,
and walk out it myself.

My self-worth,
will never come from how attractive
you found me,
or how you claimed to have found love
in the world that lies between my hips,
it will never come from your desire for
me,
or how many times you threatened to
take that away from me,
my self-worth will never be determined
by your ability to leave me in the dark,
and then convince I closed my own
eyes,
it was not on my to-do list to make you
stay,
my self-worth,
not determined by your love or lack
thereof,
but by my ability to witness your evil,
and still see the beauty of the world,
my ability to know that I am worthy of
unconditional and reciprocated love,
even if you tried to show me a million
times over,
that you believe I am not,
it is my self-worth,

why do I keep letting you determine it?

If you ever think
you've tested the boundaries enough,
well then, you're fucked,
because without fear we would not
grow,
and yes, familiarity is comforting,
but I would rather be driving 100 miles
per hour,
with the devil as my shotgun rider,
than be stuck in the same damn
corners of my mind.

I left flowers on your doorstep,
each and every day,
I got soaked on the days it was raining,
and sunburnt on the days it was too
hot,
but I knew you needed those flowers,
because they were your favorite,
I knew you wouldn't water them
and sometimes you would just throw
them away.

The flowers I kept giving you,
could never sustain life,
without you watering them,
and without you planting them to root.
So now I just leave you petals,
plucked off the flowers growing strong,
in the rich soil that is my own,
and you will not stop to realize I
stopped coming around,
until you stop to smell the roses,
and realize they are no longer there.

If you don't wake up and believe that your eyes hold the answers to the universe and that your smile can counter the weight of a million tears, then what is the fucking point?

When our song comes on shuffle,
I no longer turn it off,
instead I blast it loudly,
and scream it at the top of my lungs,
as a reminder of how good it feels,
to finally be over you.

I know I'll see you again,
sometime down the road,
and you'll look me in the eyes,
and tell me how sorry you are,
for everything,
for the scars on my heart,
for putting me through hell,
and I'll tell you it's fine,
you'll ask me if I hate you,
but, how could I?
you gave me pain that I turned into
poetry,
how could I hate you for that?

Yes, the mountains are beautiful,
but have you seen you?
and your legs that can carry you to
those peaks.
yes, the ocean is magnificent,
but have you seen you?
and the way your eyes see beauty in the
way no one else can.
yes, the sunset is amazing,
but have you seen you?
and the way your skin falls perfectly to
soak up its golden light,
the world is beautiful,
but you are part of the world,
as equally as the mountains, the ocean,
and the sun,
have you really seen you?
I don't think you have,
but I really think you should.

I used to dream about you,
I hoped we would run into each other,
in a coffee shop in 5 years,
like they say will happen in the movies,
and you'd grab my face gently,
and apologize for shattering my heart,
way back when we were too young to be
in love,
but you hate coffee,
and in 5 years I'll be living across the
world,
so, I stopped dreaming about when
you'd wake up and realize,
and started enjoying the cups of coffee
you never stayed long enough to share,
I no longer want you,
you may have been my cup of tea,
but I prefer coffee now.

You used to consume my thoughts,
my feelings,
and my body,
but now when people ask,
you were just another bad relationship.

57

I was always there to fix you when you
were broken,
so, when I was broken,
you assumed I knew how to fix myself.

We are often fooled in this life,
whether it is by models,
or celebrities,
by making us believe,
we must look a certain way,
or be loved by a certain number of
people,
but in the end,
I think the person that fools us the
most,
is ourselves,
because we spend our entire lives
convincing ourselves,
that our future is more important,
than the moments we're in right now.

I still love you,
the way I love looking back at old
photographs,
and how I feel when I listen to my
favorite song from back in 2016,
but I know that if we met now,
we probably wouldn't work,
cause we aren't young and careless,
how we were when we were 18,
we're 21 now,
and life is a little more complicated,
and we're both a little different than
who we used to be when it was us,
I play guitar now,
and kind of like beer,
you'd probably hate my new piercings,
and the way I don't shut up about living
in a van,
I think you weren't meant to love me
now,
you were only meant to love me when I
needed you,
and while I don't know who you are
anymore,
I sure loved the version of you that
needed me.

When you looked at me,
and your eyes lit up,
like you had never seen a sunshine,
like the one I gave you before,
I knew I was fucked.

One day,
a certain heartbreak will teach you that
you need to learn to be happy on your
own,
you were mine.

There are things you must experience
before you die,
and there are things you experience
that make you want to die,
I would love to learn to wrestle,
but I don't think I can,
when the thought of being pinned down,
brings me back to the dark room,
where my open legs became the answer
to your dark and closed off soul,
I would love to experience the northern
lights,
but I don't think I can,
because the beauty in the sky,
will remind me of the beauty in my
soul,
that you took from me that night,
I would love to dance,
but I don't think I can,
because my body was taken on that bed
that night,
and it has not been mine ever since,
I would love to write a book,
but I don't think I can,
because my hands tremble,
and my chest tightens up,

at the thought,
of sharing any part of me with anyone,
ever again,
I would love to sleep,
next to someone I love,
but I don't think I can,
because the thought of pretending I
have a soul to give someone,
is worse than the fact
that it's not there at all,
I would love to love you,
but I can't,
because I don't have a soul,
I don't have a body,
and my heart will never heal,
I would love to experience life,
but I can't,
because my life is not mine,
the only things that were mine,
were stripped from my existence,
on a drunk Saturday night,
I would love to experience love,
but I can't,
because I can speak,
without someone listening,
my no can mean yes,

while you slip your hands down my
body,
and take over it,
like the waves,
capturing the shore,
I would love to live,
but it's impossible,
when I am a walking corpse,
that rose from the dead,
the night that you killed me.

You cannot let bad days,
make you think you have a bad life.

Comparison is killing you,
but you're addicted to it,
maybe it's because,
pretending you could become someone
else,
is easier than learning to be yourself,
it's easy to convince yourself,
that if you just looked like them,
or had the money for their clothes,
if you had the time to do this or that,
then you would finally be happy,
it's easy to convince yourself,
that if you just had more free time,
or a better job,
or access to this or that,
then you would finally be happy,
it's harder to realize,
that it is all in your head,
that you hold your world in your hands,
and the only things making you
unhappy,
are your own thoughts,
your own perceptions,
and your own actions,
you have access to an entire world of
happiness,

it's just easier to pretend,
that it'll all fall into place,
and it's harder to realize,
that the only way it will,
is if you believe it will,
you will never look like somebody,
that isn't you,
the only person,
you get the pleasure of being is
yourself,
so, why do you spend so much time,
convincing yourself that you'd be
happier,
if you become somebody else?

Today I want to do it all,
because one day when I'm old and frail,
and my fingers can barely move,
I'll regret all of the pages of books,
that my fingers didn't turn when they
could,
and all the songs they could have
played,
on the guitar, I kept saying I would
learn,
when my legs cannot move me
anymore,
I'll wish they took me to more mountain
tops,
to the bottom of the ocean,
and to all the places I never went,
my vision will become foggy,
and I may never see another sunrise,
or witness the kindness of strangers,
when I could see all of it in true colors,
my license will be taken away,
and I won't be able to drive to the scenic
view,
or the lake front,
because I was worried about gas money,
and one day I may lose my memory,

so, the more memories I make,
the longer it'll take me to lose them,
so today I'm going to do it all,
because tomorrow,
or 50 years from now,
I may not be able to.

I shoot on film now,
so I'm glad you're no longer in the
picture,
because then,
I would have to throw away the
pictures,
when they're developed in 2 weeks,
and you've left once again,
just like you always did.

I wanted to believe it was true,
that at one point you loved me,
like I loved you,
that the way you held me,
was because I made you feel things,
and wasn't just to keep me from
leaving,
I used to want to ask you why you made
me cry so much when you claimed to
love me,
but now I guess I'm better off leaving it
unknown,
because I knew eventually my notebook
would fill up,
and I'd have to stop writing poems
about you,
I have never been good at goodbyes,
but this one is easy.

I wanted so badly to be beautiful,
so, I asked myself,
what I think of when I hear the word
beautiful,
in my mind flashed a slideshow,
of the sunsets I've seen,
from the hood of my car with people I
may never see again,
then came the rainy days,
and the music,
then there were the mountains and the
trees,
the laughter of people,
and the morning cups of coffee,
then last came everyone that I have
ever loved,
and I realized something,
things are only beautiful if they are
loved,
so instead of wanting to be the most
beautiful person in the room,
I now strive to be the most loving.

I stopped moving mountains for you,
and started climbing them for me.

You shouldn't be longing for someone that turns you into the worst version of yourself.

You will get through the fog.
you will find sunshine
and you will have so many late-night
bonfires on the beach,
you will watch so many sunsets and
sunrises and you will remember what
it's like
to feel so happy that you cry
you will ruin so many shoes from
making too many footprints,
and you will get through the fog.
you may be blinded
to the beauty of the world right now
and the light at the end of the tunnel
may be muted from your viewpoint.
but you will get through the fog.

I always found the concept strange,
that people come into your life,
and sometimes do not stay,
but are just a small part,
or that you can constantly find forever,
in random corners of the world,
I used to never be able to come to terms
with it,
the constant loss and change,
I used to think people leaving my life,
meant I was not worth staying,
but as I sat and watched the sun,
peak behind the hills,
I realized the world changes every day,
the sky will always turn beautiful
colors,
even without certain people,
it's who sees that same beauty in you,
who will always stay.

Some bridges are meant to be burned,
someone hand me a fucking lighter.

I want to say fuck you,
and hurl your name at the wind,
I want to punch and kick and scream,
I want to yell at you,
for the scars, you made in my soul,
but the only words that I can manage,
are thank you,
because the pain you brought me,
fuels the fire deep inside me,
and I keep fighting,
because of you,
so, I don't need to say fuck you,
I need to say thank you.

You deserve a sunrise to sunset kind of love.

I told myself,
a million times over again,
that I deserved better,
painted those words
in the back of my mind,
and still couldn't see the masterpiece
that they were,
it wasn't until I was swimming,
in the pools of self-doubt,
you used to drown me in,
and I felt the current,
pulling me towards the drop off,
that I realized it was you,
the heavy weight
of your poor mental health,
made it impossible to stay afloat,
and the sadness that melted off your
body,
and into my skin like lava,
was only burning me,
when you end a healthy relationship,
you'll be sad,
but when you are used,
as a drug for someone's loneliness,
only loved when they needed you,

that constant psychological abuse,
will leave you depressed,
there's a masterpiece,
painted in the back of your mind,
please telling yourself that.

It was our anniversary,
we were so happy,
you surprised me with pancake mix,
we planned to make them on Saturday,
time slipped through our fingers,
and we forgot,
we kept saying next weekend,
every weekend,
we kept promising we would do it,
when we were no longer busy,
when we weren't as stressed,
or weren't as tired,
and there the bag sat,
in the back of the cupboard for months,
listening to the rumble of the counters
that shook when our voices rose,
watching us walk past,
knowing we would keep forgetting it,
it's still there,
so are we,
but maybe those pancakes were never
meant to be made,
and we weren't meant to make it.

Ignorance was not a valid excuse,
when it came to my heart.

And I said,
let's take the sunset boulevard,
we can drive it until it's dark,
watch the sky become a painting,
and turn our bodies into silhouettes.
the burning sun,
was just a mere reflection,
of the sparks we lit inside each other,
on that warm July night,
both our minds begged mother nature,
to keep the world lit up,
but our love will never beat
the forces of nature,
but I love how much we tried,
and even though our sun has set,
I'll always be reminded of you,
when after every sunset,
I watch the sky become a gradient of
blue.

Part 1: Drowning in self-loathe

someone called me fat today,
I really couldn't believe it,
they pulled my shirt up and clenched
my stomach,
they looked me in the eyes,
and told me I was fat,
until I did believe it,
someone called me ugly today,
it caught me slightly off guard,
I didn't quite understand,
why they don't like what they saw,
how they could know everything about
me,
and still could not see,
my tears fell through my fingers like
sand,
and I finally began to understand,
someone made me cry today,
they forced the belief down my throat,
that my appearance was my value,
they convinced me,
that perfection equaled beauty,
they made me put on their vision,
so, I couldn't not see,
I wanted to stop them,
and tell them they're wrong,

but that someone,
was me.

Part 2: Swimming in self-loathe

someone called me fat today,
I really didn't believe it,
I swore I was beautiful,
the last time I checked,
their words filled my brain,
getting louder and louder,
but with the strongest of will power,
I forced them out,
someone called me ugly today,
it almost made me cry,
but I remembered everything I was,
and I eventually let their words die,
they tried to tell me again and again,
the constant pitter patter of their
teardrops on my head,
I wouldn't let them get to me,
it was my own vision of myself that
mattered,
and not what they see,
someone almost made me cry today,
they tried to force beliefs down my
throat,
but I knew my value,
would never come from my appearance,
I knew I was beautiful,
despite imperfections,

they tried so hard to show me their
vision,
an ugly,
a fat,
version of myself,
I did not want to see,
I wanted to be angry with them,
but that someone,
was me.

Part 3: Floating in self-love

someone called me beautiful today,
it made me so happy to hear,
their compliments filled my heart,
and made me smile ear to ear,
they were not bothered by my stretch
marks,
or the scars on my hips,
it did not matter my waistline,
or the size of my lips,
someone told me I was beautiful today,
they made the birds chirp a little louder,
the sun feel a little warmer,
and the sound of laughter seem a little
brighter,
everyone I passed,
seemed to smile a little wider,
and all my problems,
seemed to feel a little lighter,
they made my world more beautiful,
every little thing,
was a wonderful sight to see,
and I'm so glad to say that,
that someone was me.

You know,
of all the things that could have broken
me in this life,
it's just kind of funny
that it was you.

97

I deserve everything you made me
believe was asking too much.

I will continue to radiate
even more love,
than I was
when you told me that I love too
strongly,
I will never,
ever,
be too much for hands
that are willing to grow,
so that they can hold my overflowing
love.

Sit down,
find your seat,
be quiet and listen,
from pre-k to senior year,
interruption was my biggest fear,
don't talk when I'm talking,
don't be too loud,
so, when I saw the girl crying in the
corner,
I didn't dare make a sound,
see you preached non-violence,
but all I was ever taught was silence,
so, when the weekend came,
I was all alone,
I craved to be loved and for someone to
hold,
my phone buzzed,
It's that boy,
you know the one I drooled over in class,
he asked me to come over,
I grabbed my keys without a second
thought,
girls chase boys, right?
well that's what I was taught,
I rang the doorbell,
he seemed unenthusiastic,

we went downstairs,
he shut the door,
the only noise was the squeaky floor
board,
we sat on the couch to watch a movie,
yet five minutes in,
my face to his was all I could see,
I wanted to stop,
now let me think,
what was I taught?
he told me I'd look better wearing less,
all I knew was taking orders,
so, I started to undress,
I wanted to stop,
now let me think again,
what was I taught?
don't talk when he's talking,
do what you're told,
be quiet and listen,
now with my throat,
in his hand to hold,
he had me on lockdown,
I was his girl,
and on Instagram let's face it,
he was my world,
night after night,

it was him that was right,
and whatever I said led in to a fight,
my battered and broken body
couldn't take it anymore,
his punching bag,
was all I was for,
I finally got the nerve to tell somebody,
they sent me to a class,
I sat and took orders,
on how to say no,
on how to move on,
and on how to grow,
wait hold up,
saying no was all I needed to do?
that would make him stop?
but the answer is always silence,
yeah that's what I was taught,
I tried to say no,
I tried to speak up,
but with my head on the floor boards,
I realized he didn't give a fuck,
I went to more classes,
I tried to learn,
the strength to fight back,
was what I needed to earn,
say no,

speak up,
fight back,
yeah now that's what I got taught,
but why is it me,
who must learn a lesson,
and not the boy,
who can't calm his obsession,
I learn a lesson on how to say no,
but he needs no lesson,
on how to not have aggression,
I learn a lesson on how to speak up,
but he needs no lesson,
on how I'm not his possession,
maybe I'm wrong,
maybe I'm right,
I don't know why I should have to put up
a fight,
maybe I've grown weak,
maybe I've grown reliant,
or maybe I should have never been
taught,
to be silent.

You've found someone,
you look at the way you used to look at
me,
and one day I'll find someone,
to look at the way I looked at you,
but I'm content right now,
chasing skies that are blue.

I thought to myself.
this is my only lifetime,
when will I love myself?
in the next life,
that I don't have?
I cannot change who I am,
without being someone I am not,
why not love the skin I was given?
the heart and soul I have,
that allows me to love so deeply,
I don't want to look back,
at the only life I have,
and regret hating who I was for any of it,
this body is simply a vessel I am in,
needed for my brain to carry out tasks,
and to take my mind to the places it
wants to roam,
and for this body would mean nothing,
if it weren't for me inside of it.

I am a firm believer in speaking my mind, even if you are too afraid to listen to yours.

I didn't need to forgive you for not
calling,
I needed to forgive myself for wasting so
much time,
waiting by the phone.

He was calming like a summer nights
drive,
but horrible like a snowstorm in May,
seasons change,
but unfortunately,
people don't.

The sky still turns into a painting without you.

Life is hard,
but the fight is worth it,
when you're down,
and feeling blue,
through it all,
see yellow.

The end.

www.ingramcontent.com/pod-product-compliance
Lightning Source LLC
Chambersburg PA
CBHW072102150726
47999CB00005B/1835